CELL WARS

IN THE BEGINNING

A. MILES

ILLUSTRATED BY N. P. MONAGHAN

To my dearest Darcy

Happy reading!

All my love

Aunty Panda
x

AJMiles
x

ISBN: 1494292491
ISBN 13: 9781494292492
A CIP catalogue record for this book is available
from the British Library.

AM — For Paul, Patrick and Grace x

NPM — For Rhys and Robert x

BANDS

MASTER BASO

Capt
Neutro

MAP OF BLOOD VESSELS

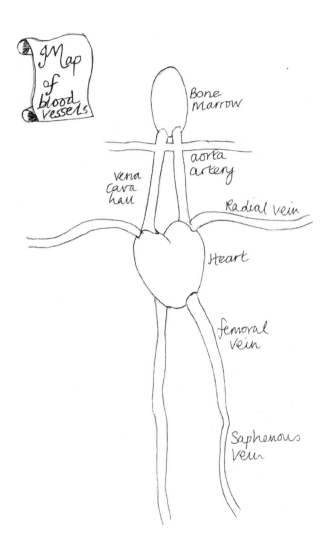

INTRODUCING

Master Baso

Captain Neutro

Bands

Commander Lympho

Captain Mono

PROLOGUE

If you were to open your mouth, you'd see a
shiny set of teeth (hopefully), a tongue and
some funny looking dangly thing at the back
of your throat. If you were to open your eyes
really wide or even pull back your eyelids
(my daughter does that and it's disgusting),
you'd see a small black circle (the pupil)
surrounded by a beautiful ring of colour (the
iris). Mine is blue. My friend's is green with

brown freckles on it. (Honestly it is!)

Now look carefully at your eyeball, the white bit. Can you see thin, reddish-pink wavy lines? These are blood vessels. They are tunnels, which carry blood around your body.

Do you know what blood looks like? Yes I know it's a red liquid. I mean do you know what it looks like up close. Really close. If you have a look at blood under a microscope, you see hundreds and hundreds of tiny red blobs all rushing along. These are called red blood cells. There are millions of them in your body. You can't see them with your eyes and you can't feel them in your body but they are there, keeping you alive.

They have help. There are some really important blood cells inside your body. You can't see or feel these either. They're white and they are slightly bigger than red blood cells. They are called white blood cells (You knew they were going to be called that, didn't you?)

Now really use your imagination to go deeper into your body. Imagine you could peel back the skin off your wrist to see the blood vessels (revolting and very messy). Pretend you have shrunk so small you can fit into one of those blood vessels. (My son says that would be epic!) You find yourself in a tunnel, next to lots of other tunnels, all curving one way or another, up and down a vast area, next to the skeleton inside your body. Hundreds of red blood cells would be swimming next to you, carrying you along in the watery plasma liquid.

Now picture yourself swimming inside one of those long, creamy bones from your skeleton. The bone has a hard outer casing but soft, spongy texture middle. This is the bone marrow and this is where all blood cells are made. Most of your bones make blood cells. As you get older (like me), its only bones like your spine, breastbone, ribs and small parts of your legs and arms that produce blood cells.

So finally you are in the bone marrow, a jellylike substance, which contains blood, fat and some very special cells. Look around and you see hundreds of white, round balls with jellyfish type legs. These are the white blood cells and they are about to start their very important job. Let's watch and see what happens.

CHAPTER 1

In the Bone Marrow, a bell rings and some of the older, white blood cells swim away, off on their mission to protect the body. Some white blood cells are left behind. They are young, white blood cells, which have just been made in the Bone Marrow. They must complete their training, before they are allowed to go on missions. They bunch together under a soft, pink, padded tissue wall, waiting for their teacher.

He glides in silently, his cloak barely making a rustle in the hushed, subdued room. All eyes are on the Master. He is legendary throughout the blood system. A slightly scary but revered teacher who knew when you were ready for active duty. Master Baso was the cell to please, to respect and most importantly to listen to.

"Good morning cells!" cried out Master Baso, his eyes scanning the room.

"Good morning Master Baso," replied all the new, young cells. Well almost all of them. One was missing.

"Where is Bands?" shouted Master Baso." He's late… again!"

✳ ✳ ✳

Bands was swimming with some red blood cells way down in the body, when he heard the Bone Marrow School bell.

"Late again?" laughed one of the red blood cells.

"As always," said Bands smiling. "I'd better go. See you later!"

Bands moved away from the group of cells. He crossed over a junction of tunnels running left and right and up and down and made his way to the Bone Marrow school. As he looked through an archway ahead, he could see his teacher talking to the new group of cells that had been made that morning. Bands floated slowly towards the back of the classroom, hoping to slip in unnoticed, his round, pale body camouflaged amongst all the other cells. It didn't work.

"Good morning Bands," Master Baso boomed over the rows of young blood cells. "So glad you could join us."

All the new cells, tightly packed together into the pocket of marrow tissue, turned to face the back. Band's face flushed bright red. "I was just explaining about the red blood cells," continued Master Baso, "and as you obviously feel you know all of this, by not arriving on time, maybe you would like to tell us instead?"

Bands sighed. He'd been at school for ages but still he wasn't allowed to advance to the next stage of training. He had to stay in the classroom because Master Baso thought he wasn't ready. Bands was convinced it was because he didn't like him.

"They are the workers. They carry oxygen from the lungs around the body and take the carbon dioxide away," said Bands in a monotonous voice.

"Is that all?" said Master Baso.

"Is that all what Sir?"

"Is that all they do or is that all you know?" continued Master Baso.

"I answered didn't I?" said Bands rudely.

All the young blood cells stared at Bands with their mouths open.

"Come, come Bands," said Master Baso. "That's not the way to enthuse our new brothers and sisters. These new cells are at the start of their life. They are eager to learn how they will take part in our fight against infections."

"But that's the problem," said Bands interrupting. "All we ever do is learn. We don't actually get involved in the fighting."

Master Baso shook his head. "Bands, you are too impatient. There is much you need to know before you become a truly great white blood cell."

Master Baso turned away from Bands and glided over the top of the new cells. "Our red blood cell cousins are many in number. There are at least 600 red blood cells for every one of us. They help to keep the human body moving, by the delivery of oxygen to all the muscles and organs." He paused and moved in closer to the eager new cells. "But we white blood cells, or as I like to call us, …the WBCs," he chuckled, as if he'd made the best joke in the world, "are the army and the ambulance crew. We fight bacteria and remove invaders. We clear away old and damaged cells by eating them and release chemicals into our human's body to help speed up the healing process."

The new cells were all watching Master Baso intently, listening to every word he said. Except for Bands. He wasn't listening. He was too busy bouncing up and down into the soft, spongy tissue beneath him.

"There are many dangers here," continued Master Baso. "A blow to the human body can cause blood vessels to burst. It is our job to eat those blood cells before they seep into the surrounding tissue." Master Baso scanned the crowd of wide-eyed white cells. "Can you think of any other dangers you might face?"

"Can we get stuck?" asked one eager cell.

"That's right!" shouted out Master Baso enthusiastically, pleased that some of his new students were listening. "We white blood cells have a nucleus in our body." All the cells peered down at their middles to have a better look.

"This nucleus has a computer system which contains lots of information, like a human's brain. And like a human's brain, we must look after it above all else. As it makes our body less flexible, it is sometimes difficult for us to move through narrow areas like the capillaries. These are the tiny tunnels at the end of veins and arteries." Master Baso looked at them sternly. "If you get stuck, your life will be over."

Band's bouncing had become more exuberant and he almost toppled over into the cell sitting next to him. The cell giggled and then straightened up when she saw Master Baso looking straight at them.

"Did you say something?" asked Master Baso, sailing right up to Bands.

"No sir. Not a word." Bands smiled.

"Hmm," said Master Baso, eyeing him suspiciously, before turning round to face the other cells. "Now, I would like to do a practice drill outside the Bone Marrow."

"Another boring drill," said Bands, pulling a face and pretending to yawn.

The cell next to him giggled again. Fortunately for Bands, Master Baso didn't hear or at least pretended not to.

CHAPTER

The new cells followed their teacher outside, bumping into each other as they went, trying to navigate the dark, narrow paths.

"I would like you to practice your

amoeboid motion," said Master Baso finding a space wide enough to demonstrate. "Watch!"

The cells stared as Master Baso's body stretched until it was wide enough to wrap around a cell. They could see his nucleus very clearly now.

"You have many weapons inside your nucleus. We want the suction gun for this task. Now you try."

The cells all began to copy him, stretching out their bodies. As they did so, their nucleus opened up and the cells could see their personal computer screen in the middle of their body. A picture of all the different weapons and command buttons flashed up on the screen and it was difficult to see the suction gun.

Suddenly a lightning bolt cracked overhead and the whole area was lit up. Now they could see the pale, pink, padded walls covered with multiple patterns. They looked like embroidered quilts. Some of the new cells flinched, their legs shaking scared by the noise and the light.

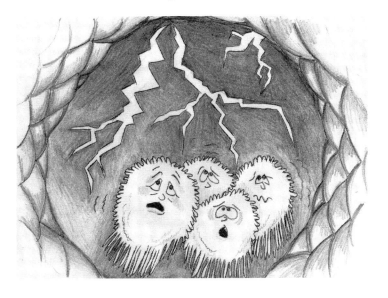

"Don't worry about those," said Master Baso, as his body snapped back to its original shape. "Happens all the time. It's because of the electricity inside the body. Nothing to worry about."

He was interrupted by a loud high-pitched noise in the tunnel. "What's happening?" shouted out the cell that had been giggling at Bands in class.

"That is a warning signal that something is wrong," answered Master Baso calmly. "Follow me!"

The younger cells moved along in the dim dark, feeling the way with their legs like a centipede. Master Baso led them down one narrow passageway after another until he finally stopped in front of a group of older, white blood cells. The young cells, not looking where they were going, all bumped into one another like falling dominoes.

"Watch!" shouted Master Baso, as the cells all jostled for the best position.

The older, white blood cell soldiers were taking orders from their superior, Commander Lympho. He was a very clever white blood cell. His nucleus was made up of many different, intelligent computer systems, which meant he knew and remembered everything.

Next to him was Captain Neutro, another highly skilled white blood cell.

Bands knew all about Captain Neutro. He was legendary. A famous 'cellebrity' who was known everywhere he went. After every mission, Captain Neutro would tell the new cells all the dangerous and exciting things that had happened in the Cell Wars. Bands thought he was the best cell in the army.

"Right. We have a code blue. I repeat a code blue," said Commander Lympho addressing the regiment. "A blood vessel has burst. We've lost quite a few red blood cells already. They've broken open and are spilling their guts everywhere. We need to contain this leak as quickly as possible."

"Have the B cells been activated?" said Captain Neutro.

"Not yet," replied Captain Mono, a white blood cell well known for her calmness and strength. "We will need to wait and see if there is any sign of infection."

"Okay," responded Commander Lympho. "This is it. You know the drill. I want this dealt with quickly."

"Yes sir!" shouted the army of white blood cells, as they hurtled off into the network of tunnels.

Captain Neutro continued to talk to Commander Lympho. Bands manoeuvred closer, so he could hear what they were saying.

"I don't have to tell you how important it is that we get this right. Report back when the situation is under control," said Commander Lympho, as he propelled himself down the tunnel back to base.

"Yes sir. Right away," replied Neutro. As he turned himself around to address Master Baso, he saw Bands right behind him, standing to attention. "Okay Bands. Tell me! What emergency are we talking about?"

"Sir! Our human has developed a bruise and we need to contain the leaking blood," said Bands.

"Very good," Neutro said. He looked over at Master Baso. "I think he might be ready, Sir?"

Master Baso slowly nodded his head in approval. "Remember what I have taught you Bands and be careful."

Neutro turned to Bands. "Would you like to go with me?"

"Yes sir!" said Bands triumphantly. Finally he was going on a mission.

CHAPTER

Bands stayed behind Neutro as they raced
to the site of the burst blood vessel in the
elbow. Teams of white blood cells had

spread themselves across the Radial vein
to surround the bleeding area. Neutro and
Bands joined them.

Slowly they began the amoeboid
motion, commanding their bodies to
stretch open and digest the broken red
blood cells. Then they needed to activate
the nucleus weapon.

Bands looked at his computer screen.
Scanning through the data, he found

the button S1. As he pressed it, a panel underneath the computer screen opened up and a cylindrical pipe shot out. This was the suction gun. Bands could feel the gun pulling the cell into his nucleus to be neutralized. It was a very strange feeling. Having completed this task, he moved onto finding another cell.

Bands and the rest of the white cells continued like this for an hour until finally the leak was contained. The WBCs (white blood cells), feeling they could burst at any second, now began the next part of the operation. They pressed the communication function button C2 on their computer screen to launch the release of different chemicals from their nucleus.

Bands watched as the chemicals poured out of the same panel that the gun had appeared from earlier. These chemicals swam down the vein tunnel. They were messengers whose job was to summon new red blood cells to the area.

"What happens now?" said Bands, exhausted and feeling extremely full.

"Now we watch and wait," Neutro replied.

Almost immediately, new red blood cells flooded into the area and swam into the surrounding tissue walls, making them puff up.

"What happens now?" asked Bands.

"Do you see the green molecules above?" said Neutro. Bands looked at the tiny green pieces floating above his head. "That is the result of the blood breaking up. It changes colour from purple to green. Then they will start to turn yellow and then dissolve completely into the bloodstream," said Neutro. "Finally it gets carried off in the tunnels to the liver and kidneys for processing and eventual banishment."

"You mean when our human goes for a wee," laughed Bands.

"Yes, very funny!" Neutro smiled.

"And a poo!" continued Bands.

"Okay, you know how the human body works," laughed Neutro, "and now you know how a bruise works. Do you think you could handle that next time?"

"Yes sir!" Bands said confidently. "Easy!"

"Okay, okay," said Neutro turning himself around. "Don't get too carried away. Looks like our job is done here. I need to debrief

Commander Lympho and you need to go back to school. Do you remember how to get back?"

Bands nodded glumly.

"Come on Bands," encouraged Neutro. "You'll get to do this everyday soon enough. But first you have to go to school." And with that he sped off down the tunnel, leaving Bands alone.

How he wished he could go with him. He was sure he would learn a lot more if he were allowed to ride around with Neutro all day.

He made his way back up the slow moving Radial vein tunnel, with all the other deflated red cells, that were now going to pick up more oxygen from the lungs. He travelled through the right side of the heart and then into the left side. He saw the tunnel crossing into the Bone Marrow, next to the great Aorta artery. He hesitated. He didn't want to go to school and listen to the Master telling him about the dangers, especially after this morning.

"I'm not going to learn anymore in school," he said defiantly. "I'm ready for active duty. I'll show them." So Bands went down the Aorta artery instead of going back to the Bone Marrow school.

CHAPTER

As Bands crawled along, bolts of lightning flashed and the whole area lit up in front of him. This was so exciting here in the middle of the action and adventure. He could see the pink tunnels, shiny and wet, full of red blood cells all carrying oxygen in their bodies. Hundreds of bright, red, spherical discs went past him, like surfers riding the waves in the sea.

"Hi Bands!" called out one of the red blood cells swimming next to him. "Where you off to?"

"Nowhere in particular. Just looking," Bands replied.

"Just looking! That's a good one," laughed the blood cell. "Sure you're not looking for trouble! Anyway slow coach. Gotta go. I have a wave to catch."

Bands smiled as he watched him speed off in the current in the artery. Then the lightning shots stopped and it was dark again.

Bands didn't like the dark. It's not that he was scared. Bands wasn't scared of anything. He just couldn't remember where to go. He would bump into the walls of the tunnels and miss the exits. He would find himself going down a vein tunnel that led to the heart rather than up an artery passageway that went to the muscles and organs in the body. It was his fault. He should know the Blood system route by now but he never concentrated in class. He was too busy dreaming of all the dangerous missions he would do, when he was allowed to.

In the dark, Bands could hear the cracks and crackles, the bursts and claps of the huge blood river system he was part of. He could feel the tunnel walls vibrating from the pulsing heart and the blood cells whirring past him in the straw coloured, plasma water. Then once again the giant chamber was filled with flickering lightning, like a huge fireworks display. It was like this all the time in the network of tunnels. Lights on. Lights off. Lights on again.

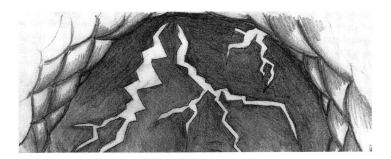

Bands moved along following a group of red blood cells. In the artery, it was the heart that pumped the blood along. It was a fast ride and there was no way of turning back. Red blood cells swam past, bumping and pushing him along, next to the thick, muscular walls.

The artery began to break off into smaller tunnels. Bands knew this was where he should stop. He wasn't allowed to go any further. Not into the small capillary tunnels. Not on his own. Not yet. These were very thin and fragile passages, only one cell thick and you had to carefully navigate your way through. He couldn't join a group of blood cells and get pushed along.

"I know I'm not supposed to but it doesn't look that difficult," said Bands to himself, "and who would know?"

Bands breathed in and squeezed his body into the capillary tunnel. He edged his way along in the darkness. There were no lights, no lightning bolts, no cracks and claps. It was silent, except for the faraway drone of the beating heart. 'It's a lot darker in here?' thought Bands, who was beginning to wonder if this wasn't such a good idea after all.

Suddenly he stopped moving. He pressed his body forwards but nothing happened. He pushed his legs out as far as they would go. Again nothing. It was as though he was stuck to something. He was being held in place by a force far greater than he had ever known and to make matters worse, he didn't know where he was. 'Oh no! How am I going to get out of this?'

CHAPTER

Bands pressed all his legs down really hard
for the third time. Still he couldn't move.
He felt the thick walls of cushioned tissue

surrounding him, cocooning his body.

"I must be stuck in a muscle!" Bands said to himself. "If I don't get out of this, I'm going to die." The walls of the muscle started to squeeze his body. Each squeeze sucked him deeper into the tunnel wall, swallowing him like a snake devouring a mouse. In a few more minutes, his short life as a white blood cell would be over.

"Come on Bands, think!" he shouted out loud.

He had to get into a connecting vein tunnel before it was too late. Bands remembered Master Baso talking about the white blood cell's energy. Their nucleus was not only for the weapons, but also controlled their speed and strength. He opened up his nucleus and studied the information on the computer screen. There were so many functions. Where was the control button for the power? He couldn't see it! There were too many control buttons. He felt his body once more squeezed further into the tunnel wall and then he saw the P1 button. He hit it. Just in time.

Bands stretched out his body and legs with all the power he could generate, until he heard a sound like a Wellington boot being pulled out of mud. Finally he was free but the force of the suction sent him spinning out of control. Bands tried to straighten up but he was spinning too fast. He was being turned around and around. He was pushed and spun in all directions, his speed increasing with each new push.

He was spun to the right. Then he lurched to the left. Bouncing backwards off a wall he was sent shooting forwards down another tunnel, a wider tunnel than before. He span around and around at great speed until finally he crashed into something or someone!

"What are you doing here?" a voice shouted.

Bands was still dizzy from the spinning but recognized the voice straight away. It was

Captain Neutro. "I ran into some trouble back in the capillaries Sir!" explained Bands, trying to straighten up.

"You've been told to stay out of the capillaries. You're not ready to travel on your own yet!" shouted an angry Neutro.

Bands looked down at the floor or tried to, as his head was still dizzy from all the spinning around.

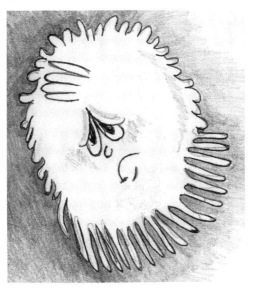

"I didn't get to be the blood cell I am today without going to school. Taking part, listening and practising is how you learn Bands!" Neutro lowered his voice and looked at Bands sympathetically. "Master Baso is a brilliant teacher. There aren't many like him. You doing this is why he's holding you back from operations! Now I'm taking you back to school and you need to apologise to Master Baso."

"Oh but…" said Bands before deciding it would be better to be quiet.

Bands reluctantly followed Neutro back to the Bone Marrow. He knew he had let Neutro down which was bad enough, but now Master Baso would have extra ammunition to throw at him. This was going to be horrible.

CHAPTER 6

Master Baso was discussing the Code Blue operation from that morning, when Bands joined the group of young cells.

"And where have you been?" bellowed Master Baso.

"I. I..had something to do Sir," mumbled Bands.

"Speak up, speak up," said Master Baso.

"I had something to do Sir!"

"Something important?" asked his teacher, studying Bands face very carefully.

"Yes Sir!"

"Well do tell us. We are very interested to know what was so important you decided it was necessary to miss your lessons!"

"I thought I heard a danger signal," Bands lied, looking down at the spongy tissue floor. "I decided to try and help."

"And did you?"

"Did I what Sir?"

"Did you help?"

"Not exactly Sir," said Bands, who realised Master Baso wasn't going to let him get away with this.

"Well, what exactly did you do?" asked Master Baso.

"First of all I went down the artery and then I heard a danger signal further down the tunnel. So I decided to explore and found a blood cell that was stuck, Sir," said Bands still looking at the floor.

"So you went down into the capillary tunnel, even though you are not supposed to and tried to help another cell in a tunnel which is only one cell thick. Thereby putting yourself and the other cell at risk. Now how did you suppose that you were going to be able to help?" said Master Baso.

Bands was silent. He couldn't talk his way out of this. Master Baso knew he was lying.

His teacher shook his head as he turned away from Bands.

"As we have all just heard from young Bands here, the pathways are many and it is all too easy to get caught up with the exciting ride. But you must think about where you are going and why. Only respond to a call for help when you have support. You do not need to go looking for danger. There is danger all around us."

Master Baso continued with the lesson, gliding up and down the rows of cells. "Who is our enemy?" he asked.

"Bacteria and viruses are our enemy!" cried out the young cells.

"Good. It is important that you do not underestimate how deadly they can be. Bacteria are very small and clever. They can reproduce themselves and divide at

an alarming rate, first two, then four,
then eight and so on. Please look at the
whiteboard."

All the students looked at a picture of the
bacteria splitting in two and making more of
themselves.

"You need to be aware of all that is around you at all times. If bacteria are allowed to multiply, they become more powerful and can take over the body, damaging the body's organs. Your quick reaction to a bacteria break out could be the difference between our human living and dying. And if our human begins to die then so do we all."

Master Baso said the last line so quietly, the cells all had to lean forward to hear him. His students all stared, transfixed on their teacher, hardly daring to breathe.

"You!" shouted Master Baso, shattering the silence and causing the cells to lose their balance and topple into one another. He was pointing at a young cell positioned on the front line. "If you heard the signal of a code red situation, five short pitched sounds and then a long drone, what would you do first?"

Master Baso got so close, the young white blood cell could see right through his teacher's body into his multiple eyed nucleus.

The young blood cell, frightened by Master Baso's outburst, began to stutter. "I…I… think I would… I think …first.."

"Come on. We haven't got all day. Think! Five short ones and a long drone."

Just then, they all heard what Master Baso had been trying to explain. Five short high-pitched sounds and then the long drone. A code red signal! It was unmistakable.

"You mean like that Sir," said another front line cell.

"Yes young cell. Exactly like that," said Master Baso, changing from teacher to commander in an instant. He opened up his nucleus to read the information on his computer screen.

"Right. This is not a drill. We have a Code Red. I repeat a Code Red. A bacterium has been spotted in the bloodstream. We need to wait for further information as to location but I think this could be a good learning experience for you all. I must attend straight away so I'd like you to attach yourselves to an older WBC and watch what they do. Please stay with your superior. At the moment we don't know what kind of bacteria this is or where it is. Be safe out there!"

Master Baso flew off, leaving the 30 young WBCs looking at each other. Bands knew this was his opportunity.

"Come on then!" shouted Bands, taking charge. "You heard what he said. Let's go!"

CHAPTER

Bands led the young group of cells to the meeting point. A huge army of WBCs surrounded Commander Lympho and

Captain Neutro. A large vein map was projected on the tissue wall behind them.

"Captain Neutro would you run through the operation?" Commander Lympho asked.

"Look at your screens now," Neutro ordered the WBCs. Bands and the rest of the cells opened up their nucleus to see their computer screens. They saw a digital image of the Cocci bacteria, alongside its description.

"We have discovered the Cocci bacteria has entered the bloodstream near the saphenous vein," said Neutro. "This invader got in through a cut in the outer casing near the knee. There are two parts to this operation. The first is to find and destroy all the bacteria. The second is to secure the opening in the outer casing with a scab."

"I want the T cell team deployed to this position," Commander Lympho said, pointing to the map. Then he turned to Captain Neutro and asked, "Is there anything else that we need to be careful of?"

"We need to act fast," said Neutro. "They are already duplicating themselves and cell division will be rapid."

"Okay cells. You know what to do. Move out," barked the Commander.

The WBCs drove out in pairs into the tunnel system, like the animals going into the ark, each new cell attached to a more experienced, older white cell. Bands had managed to attach himself to Neutro, locking into his body like two Lego pieces joined together.

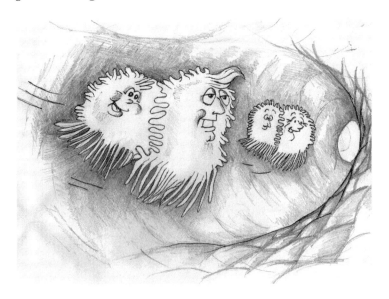

"Sir, why is this Cocci bacteria dangerous?" Bands asked Neutro as they sped along the tunnels.

"All bacteria can be harmful to the body. The Cocci is normally one we can deal with if we get to it quickly. The quicker they are to duplicate themselves the harder it is for us to destroy them. This one causes nasty skin infections like boils or Impetigo. Some of them are more deadly and if we don't get to them in time, they can eat away human flesh."

"Yuk! That's disgusting!" said Bands, pulling a face.

"I know but it's all part of our job. Hang on!" shouted Neutro, increasing his speed down the long, curved, padded passageway.

Riding along in the flow of the plasma and red blood cells, Neutro felt a rush of excitement. He knew it would be dangerous but he couldn't wait to be a part of it.

The WBCs who had gone on ahead were sending information via their cell phones. They warned that the bacteria were increasing rapidly and invading the tissues and bloodstream. Neutro and the other WBCs moved as fast as they could, never stopping or hesitating. But it was difficult. There was a heaviness in the plasma that made every push forward feel as though a great force was driving them back, like they were in a wind tunnel.

"It feels like it's getting hotter?" Bands shouted.

"I'm afraid the temperature will continue to rise because of the heat we are generating and the chaos the bacteria are causing," Neutro shouted back. "I'm hoping it's not much further."

They turned left, then right and then left again. Along the tunnels they went and then there was a sharp turn. Bands clung on tight. He'd never gone this fast before.

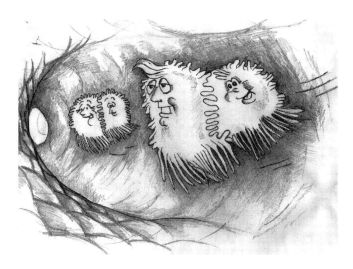

Up ahead, Bands could see lots of WBCs all grouped together in front of Captain Mono. Neutro pulled up alongside.

"It seems the situation is worse than we thought," Captain Mono said. "The numbers of bacteria are into the hundreds and the WBCs who got here earlier have been doing their best to eat them but are being driven back by the sheer force of their numbers. We need to surround as many as we can and cut them off. Especially the ones at the front who are racing towards the heart."

"How close are they?" asked Neutro.

"Close enough," said Captain Mono. "We've asked for backup. The marrowbone is producing up to 120,000 new blood cells a second."

"Okay cells. This is it," said Captain Neutro, addressing the troop. Lights flashed in the tunnel once more. "We have to go down the femoral vein. Once in position, get in as close as you can. Good luck."

Hundreds of WBCs darted away like arrows shot from bows. Neutro and Bands joined the rush of cells. They raced down the rippled tunnels, branching left and right. The blood flow here in the veins was much slower than in the pulsing arteries. They also had to navigate through the valves, large doors, which opened up to let you into the next part of the tunnel. Once through you could not go back.

Over the cell sound system, they heard the countdown to reaching their destination. 10,9,8,7,6,5,4,3,2,1.

As Neutro and Bands joined the meeting point where the white blood cells were all gathered, the tunnel was illuminated with a blinding flash of light and then they saw them. The place was crawling with bacteria.

"That's the Cocci bacteria," said Neutro, moving his 50 WBCs into a position on the west side of the tunnel, where they could

watch the bacteria's movement more closely.
The round shaped invaders rushed through
the tunnel, causing chaos as they went.

"Look at that one," shouted Bands. "It's
splitting in two." Bands was afraid there were
too many to exterminate.

"They become angrier and more deadly,
the longer they are in the blood system.
When you see their faces change, you will
know it's serious," said Neutro.

Just then Captain Neutro's cell phone rang. Bands continued to watch the trespassers multiplying in the tunnels like bubbles popping up in boiling liquid.

Neutro addressed the cells. "That was Captain Mono. Her team is positioned on the east side of the tunnel. We are on the west. This two-pronged attack means we can surround the bacteria to ensure none of them escape," Neutro explained.

"But the backup team aren't here yet," said Bands.

"We will have to start without them. You know what you have to do. Get ready to attack. On my count 3,2,1, charge!"

Bands looked at Captain Neutro. He had been waiting his whole life for this moment. Going into battle, attacking his enemies is what he had dreamed about. Now, he wasn't so sure. But he was a soldier and he had been born to do this.

"Yes Sir!" he answered bravely and they charged ahead.

CHAPTER 8

Neutro, Bands and the rest of the team flew into the path of the bacteria and the red blood cells, bobbing up and down in the plasma. Bands watched Neutro begin his chase on one of the bacteria. Being much smaller than Neutro, it could dart around the red blood cells more quickly. Neutro pressed a button in his nucleus to activate his cellophane visor screen. This helped him lock into the bacterium's movement.

At high speed, Neutro flew after him, his body spreading out as he turned corners, first one way and then another. Bands could see the bacterium was staring to tire and run out of space.

A light flashed on Neutro's visor screen and a high-pitched beep informed him that the invader was within range.

"I have him locked down," shouted Neutro over the cell phone sound system. "Preparing to shoot!" Neutro's nucleus opened up and a venom gun appeared from the underneath the panel.

Neutro pounced and shot poisonous venom into the bacterium's body to paralyse it. Stretching out his segmented body, he sucked the enemy into his nucleus. Then he moved swiftly onto chasing the next bacterium and shooting it with the same toxic poison. Another one exterminated.

"You okay?" he managed to shout to Bands, who had started to chase a bacterium down the tunnel.

"I think I'm beginning to understand this," replied Bands as he stretched out each segment of his body like a caterpillar and disappeared round a bend. Using his cellophane visor screen, just as Neutro had done, he waited until the light and high-pitched beep informed him that the enemy was in the line of fire and locked down.

"Ok. I have him locked down. Preparing to shoot!" As Bands surrounded the invader, he pointed his venom gun at the target and shot the toxic poison. Then swiftly he changed weapons for the suction gun to pull the bacteria into his nucleus. When that was done he moved onto finding his next enemy.

The WBCs continued this way for an hour, moving into different areas once the danger had been exterminated.

"It's all clear," Bands reported back to Neutro, after finishing his last sweep of the area.

"Good," responded Neutro. "I need to call this in."

"Captain Mono," Neutro called out down his cell phone. "What is our position?"

Bands and the rest of the team listened into the conversation over the cell phone sound system.

"I think we're winning," Captain Mono answered. "The femoral and saphenous veins are virtually clear but I've had reports from a WBC near the wound site, that the scab isn't being formed quickly enough and more bacteria have got in."

"Are you okay to finish off there?" Neutro asked.

"Yes. Reinforcement is on its way and I think we have most of it under control," Mono said calmly.

"Right. I'll take my team to the wound site and inform Commander Lympho. I'll see you back at base. Over and out."

Neutro, Bands and the rest of the team sped off down the smooth femoral vein.

"Come in Commander Lympho," said Neutro down his cell phone.

"Captain Neutro," answered the Commander. "What do you have to report?"

"The outbreak of bacteria is now contained in the veins. Captain Mono is controlling the

WBCs there. The main problem now is the outbreak at the wound site. More bacteria are getting through the cut as the scab isn't formed yet."

They all heard Commander Lympho pause before answering. "I need you to organize a team to clear up the dead cells and get that scab made as quickly as possible."

"Yes sir," Neutro responded. "We are on our way."

Without wasting any time, Neutro and his team fled down the vein and soon reached the wound. This area was like a large airplane hangar. Thousands of red blood cells were swimming around, while hundreds of white blood cells were continuing to attack the bacteria still pouring through the hole in the ceiling.

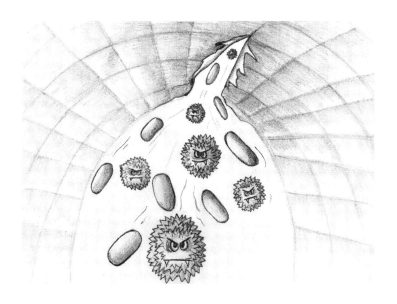

Bands had never seen anything like this. In front of him were different blood cells that looked just like fragments of a broken china plate. These pieces floated up towards the wound site where they were sticking together, covering the opening of the wound like a giant plaster.

"Those are platelets," Neutro said, as Bands gazed up at the skin ceiling. "They form a scab or plug as quickly as they can, to stop the bacteria and viruses from getting into the blood system."

"This is epic!" replied Bands.

"And necessary," said Neutro. "This job has to be done two or three times a day with some humans, especially the small ones. They seem to fall over a lot!"

Neutro moved around the wound site, assessing the situation.

"There are a lot of dead cells here," he told his team. "We need to clear these away quickly, as they are slowing down the repair job on the scab."

Bands followed orders to begin the cleanup operation with another group of young WBCs. Together they ate up the dead cells.

Neutro and the older soldiers continued to attack the bacteria. The WBCs were getting tired now as they had been fighting for hours. They had killed hundreds of the bacteria but still more were getting in, constantly multiplying and heading onwards into the blood system. When the bacteria were near the skin's surface they couldn't cause much damage but if they burrowed deeper, nearer the important organs in the human's body, like the heart and lungs, their army would become more powerful and dangerous.

"Keep going," Neutro said to the soldiers, trying to keep morale up. "It can't be for much longer now."

Bands sucked up another dead cell and digested it in his nucleus. He was very tired and wasn't sure how much longer he could continue.

Bands stopped to rest for a moment and looked around. As he did so, he saw a stream of red blood cells flowing onwards to the main vein. But there was something odd about the way they were moving. They seemed to be clumping together and hiding something in the middle of them.

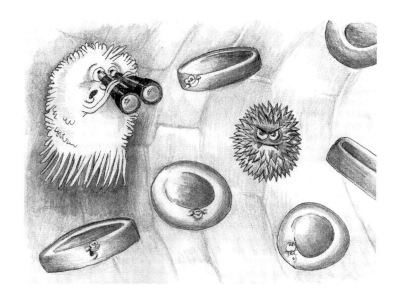

Bands opened up his nucleus and took
out his cellescopic binoculars. Zooming in, he
focused on the thick cluster of cells. When he
looked more closely, he saw the angry faces of
the round shaped Cocci invaders, but something
else worried him more. As the red blood cells
branched off towards another tunnel he finally
saw it. This wasn't the Cocci bacteria. This was a
different one. He had to warn Neutro and fast.

CHAPTER

Neutro and Bands were hiding in one
of the cushioned folds of the tunnel.
Hundreds of blood cells swam past them,

oblivious to their stakeout position. Neutro zoomed in on the new invaders with his cellescopic binoculars.

"You're right Bands!" said Neutro. "This is the Bacilli, a really clever little bacterium. Those rotating tails on the bacteria help them move quickly in the fluid, like a boat's propellers in the water. It's a good thing you saw them when you did," warned Neutro, getting out his cell phone.

"Why?" asked a curious Bands.

"This bacteria is called Tetanus. It creates painful spasms in the body and makes the muscles rigid. This can cause problems swallowing or breathing and in some cases it can cause our human to die."

Bands could tell this was serious from the tone of Neutro's voice. How many of these invaders had already got into the blood system? How far had they gone?

Neutro phoned the Commander from their viewing point. Bands listened in.

"How did you do?" the Commander asked. Neutro told him what he had seen. For a moment the Commander was quiet and then he said, "We need to bring in the

Antibodies. These are dangerous. I will activate the B cells immediately. Good work captain Neutro," he added and then he ended the call.

Neutro and Bands slipped quickly away from their position and began to round up the team of white blood cells.

"Open up your screens," ordered Neutro. Bands and the rest of the team looked down at the computer screen in their nucleus. They studied the digital image of the Bacilli bacterium, a spherical, rod shaped invader.

"Our job is to keep destroying the Cocci bacteria whilst leaving this new bacteria to the Antibodies. They are too dangerous for us and we wouldn't be able to contain them. The Antibodies are the professionals but we must not under any circumstances get in their way. They are like robots. Trained to kill according to the information they receive. If we are with the bacteria, they might think we are the enemy and kill us. Is that clear?" Neutro said to the tired looking group of white blood cells in front of him.

"Yes Sir," they answered.

"Now spread out so you have a clear view. There is a lot going on here and mistakes will be costly and life threatening. Are we ready?" asked Neutro.

"Yes Sir," they all answered, even though like Bands, they were not feeling ready at all. They took up their positions at either side of the tunnel and waited for the command to attack. Bands spotted one of the Bacilli bacteria and then another and another, all intermingled in the stream of the dark, round Cocci bacteria and red blood cells.

Suddenly there was a rumbling in the distance. A low buzz could be heard and it was getting closer. The WBCs looked up and saw small cells in large groups, flying above, like groups of helicopters.

"Who are they?" Bands asked.

"They are the Antibodies," answered Captain Neutro proudly. "These guys are tough soldiers. You see their Y shape. They have suckers on the end which means they can clamp themselves to the outside wall of the bacteria."

"Wow!" said Bands, who couldn't stop staring. "Look at them move."

The Antibodies flew in. They looked like a throng of dragonflies hovering over a river. The bottom of their cylindrical shape housed the tracking system, which helped them to find the bacteria. Bands watched one of them lock into a bacterium, fly up to it and land with its Y shaped body firmly stuck to the enemy's body. While attached, the Antibody shot the poison in, to paralyse the bacteria. Then Bands saw another Antibody doing the same thing. Within seconds, the invader was covered in Antibodies, like a swarm of bees around an orange. Moments later, a different group of white blood cells swooped in.

"They are the Exit team," explained Neutro. "Their job is to carry the paralysed enemy away in the plasma, freeing the Antibodies to fly off and capture their next invader." Neutro saw Bands worried face. "I told you there would be a lot going on. You must be careful."

"I will," promised Bands. He couldn't make any mistakes now. This was for real.

"There is no time to lose. Good luck everyone." And then Neutro gave the order.

Hearing the command to attack they charged ahead and began their assault. Bands raced to the front with five other WBCs. Locking into a Cocci bacterium, his body

stretched revealing his nucleus and computer
screen. He selected the venom gun, locked in
and open fired. "Got him!" he said out loud.

Swiftly, Bands sucked the bacterium
into his nucleus with the suction gun and
snapped back into shape before continuing
to chase the next enemy in his path.

He dived around one corner and the next
and then saw another bacterium up ahead.

Using his visor screen, Bands locked into the coordinates of the enemy and pulled out his venom gun. He fired, just as a WBC appeared in front of the bacterium. Bands had already open fired before this WBC realized what was happening.

"Get out of the way!" Bands shouted. But it was too late. The poison from the venom gun hit the WBC. Bands could only watch as the white blood cell fell to the ground paralysed. It was the giggly cell from earlier that day.

He swam towards her not realizing that he had already opened up his nucleus and the suction gun was in his hand. Bands felt the pull and then the realization of what was happening hit him. The giggly cell was being sucked towards him. Soon she would be digested in his nucleus.

"Hit the power button!" shouted Neutro, who had just seen what had happened.

Bands was bewildered and felt like he was in a dream. He didn't know what to do.

"Hit the power button!" Neutro shouted again.

This time Bands heard him and quickly pressed the switch. The force of the pull subsided just in time. Bands looked down at the frightened, giggly cell that had been rescued from the edge of elimination. "You okay?" he shouted to her.

"I can't move," she said.

Bands was so upset to see her lying lifeless like this but he knew he had to leave her and carry on. "Back up will be here soon but I've got to go."

"Don't worry. I'm fine," she said smiling, even though Bands saw she was terrified. "Not so boring now is it?"

Bands shook his head ashamed, remembering how he had acted that morning. "I've got to go. We still have so much to do but stay safe." And with that he shot off down the nearest tunnel.

CHAPTER 10

Bands now knew that he had to be really careful opening fire. There were so many of them in the tunnels and it was difficult to see clearly. When this mission started it felt like a game. As long as he was shooting at the bad guys that was all that mattered. He didn't think that one of his team could get injured or even die. Bands shuddered at the thought. He had messed up again. But he didn't have time to think about this now. He would have to deal with the consequences later.

He raced on ahead until he came to a junction. The lightning bolts lit up the area. Over on the left hand side tunnel, Bands saw the red blood cells making their way up the vein tunnel. There were no WBCs around. It looked like this area was clear. Then out of the corner of his eye, Bands noticed a shadow projected on the tissue wall. It wasn't the shape of a red blood cell. It was rod shaped!

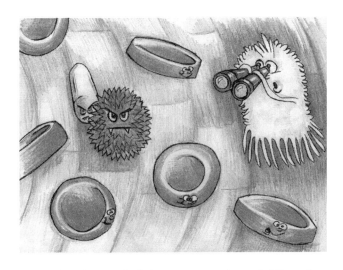

Bands chased this group of red blood cells as fast as he could. They were moving very quickly towards the heart and he was certain there was something hiding in between them. Bands followed closely behind, not wanting this enemy to spot him. These bacteria were very devious and deadly. They needed to be stopped.

As he raced through the tunnel, Bands pulled out his cellescopic binoculars. Zooming in, he could see clearly that he was right. There were more Bacilli bacteria here. He opened up his nucleus and got out his cell phone.

"What is your exact position?" asked Captain Mono, on the other end of the phone.

Bands looked at his location chart on the computer screen. "Am sending it to you now," replied Bands.

"Great work Bands," said Captain Mono. 'They must have broken free from the main crowd in all the confusion. I am sending the location coordinates to the Antibodies now but stay with the enemy. Don't lose them. Over and out."

Bands continued to follow this dangerous gang. He felt helpless. He really wanted to attack the Bacilli bacteria himself but he knew this wasn't his call to make. It wasn't his job. Then he heard the low buzz of helicopters. Suddenly lightning bolts lit up the area in front of him and he saw them, the Antibodies flying in. They'd made it.

They swooped in, attached themselves to the Bacilli bacteria and paralyzed them. Exit cells carried the bacteria away. Neutro and his team of WBCs raced up to Bands.

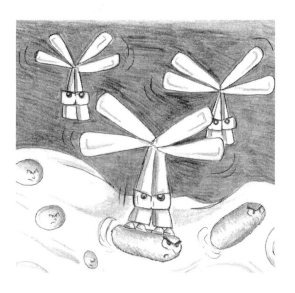

"Well done Bands," congratulated Neutro. "That couldn't have been easy for you. Sometimes we have to leave things to others. Okay, let's go and get the rest of those troublemakers."

The WBCs chased and consumed the last of the Cocci bacteria. Young blood cells cleared away the dead cells. Other cells carried the poisons, that had been produced during the fighting, back to the kidneys. The WBCs continued to consume all the Cocci bacteria while the Antibodies continued their search for the Bacilli bacteria. There was a crash of thunder and more lightning bolts. The fight continued for hours and hours.

Hours turned into days. The WBCs were exhausted. Bands wanted to rest but it wasn't over. Then finally a loud signal, a trumpeting flourish, filled the tunnels. Bands turned around to see a procession of different WBCs called Suppressor cells, swimming into the area telling everyone the good news. "Stop the fighting! Stop the fighting. The bacteria have been destroyed."

Bands stopped and looked around. It was true. There were no more bacteria. The enemy had finally been defeated.

"We did it!" shouted Captain Neutro, as the troops gathered round him.

"How many did we kill?" called out one of the WBCs.

"We won't know until the final tally later. What's important is that we worked as a team and all the invading bacteria have been stopped. Good job everyone. Now back to base for a well deserved rest."

"Captain Neutro," asked Bands, looking at the floor. "About the other day when I accidently shot at the WBC."

"Bands, she's fine. Still shaken but she's going to recover. The poison needs a couple of days to leave her system. It wasn't your fault, you know." Bands looked up at Neutro. "These things happen all the time. The more action you see, the more you realize. Now stop worrying and go and rest. That's an order!"

"Yes Sir!" replied Bands.

* * *

Later on, the troops of cells were all summoned to the great Hall of the Vena

Cava. Commander Lympho himself stood in front of them to address the crowd.

"Today has been a great day. Enemies who attempted to destroy our environment have been exterminated. We know this will not be the last day of the attacks and we know the next one will be just as difficult. We must remember that alone we are not important but together we are an army of cells, a creator of life and a phenomenal force. We are the white blood cells!"

Every cell cheered. They knew they had the best job in the human body.

✳ ✳ ✳

"You did an excellent job!" Neutro said to Bands later on. "If it hadn't been for you we might not have spotted that Bacilli bacteria until it was too late. I think you'll make a fine white blood cell soldier."

Bands flushed with pride. He had helped his fellow cells and realized the importance of looking and listening. Master Baso was right. He didn't need to go looking for danger.

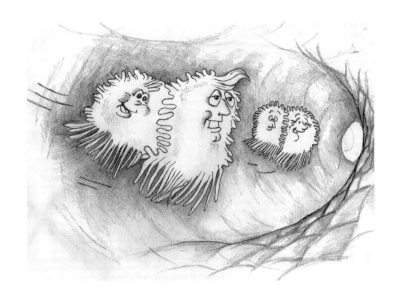

"Come on!" Neutro said. "It's back to work." And off they went, down the river of life, always alert and ready for the next battle.

GLOSSARY — USEFUL WORDS

antibody – a special protein that helps destroy or neutralize enemies

artery – a vessel that carries blood with oxygen away from the heart

bacteria – a tiny creature with one cell. Some bacteria cause infections.

band cell – a very young WBC that has recently been made in the bone marrow

blood – contains white and red cells and platelets floating in a liquid called plasma

bloodstream – the body's transport system

bone marrow – a thick spongy tissue in the middle of bones

capillary – a tiny blood vessel between the artery and vein

cell – a very small living thing. All living things are made up of cells.

energy – the power that makes things work

force – a push or a pull

molecules – tiny pieces made up of atoms (that everything is made of)

nucleus – the central, most important part of a cell

organ - part of the body (heart, kidneys, liver, lungs)

plasma – a yellowish liquid

platelets – blood cells which help blood to clot

tissue – a group of cells that stick together

vein – vessel that carries blood without oxygen back to the heart

white blood cell – neutrophil, basophil, lymphocyte and **monocyte** – fight infection in the body

5910546R00066

Printed in Great Britain
by Amazon.co.uk, Ltd.,
Marston Gate.